nickelodeon

SpongeBob SQUAREPANTS

BOOK OF EXCUSES

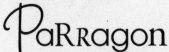

PaRragon

Bath · New York · Singapore · Hong Kong · Cologne · Delhi
Melbourne · Amsterdam · Johannesburg · Shenzhen

Table of Contents

BOOK OF EXCUSES

Excuses, Excuses

Mr Krabs: Why did you bring your pet snail to work with you?

SpongeBob: He needs to come out of his shell.

Mrs Puff: Why don't you get As and Bs?

SpongeBob: I want to be a "sea" student!

Mr Krabs: Why did you miss work yesterday?

Squidward: I didn't miss it at all!

SpongeBob's Top Ten Homework Excuses

I don't have my homework because:

1. My slug ate it.

2. Patrick drooled on it.

3. Pearl spilled Kelpo on it.

4. Plankton stole it. (He thought it was the Krabby Patty recipe.)

5. Sandy karate-chopped it.

6. It was eaten by Nematodes.

7. It was swallowed by giant clams.

8. It was sucked into my reef blower.

9. Mermaidman zapped it with his laser button.

10. My bubble buddy borrowed it and never gave it back.

SpongeBob: There were two cookies in the jar last night, and this morning there's only one. How do you explain that?

Patrick: It was so dark, I guess I missed it!

Mrs Puff: Why did you go jellyfishing instead of writing your book report?

SpongeBob: Book report? I thought you said, "Brook report!"

Mr Krabs: Why do you keep stealing the Krabby Patty recipe?

Plankton: I'd buy it from you, but I'm a little short.

SpongeBob's ⭐Top Ten⭐ Excuses for Flunking the Driving Exam Again

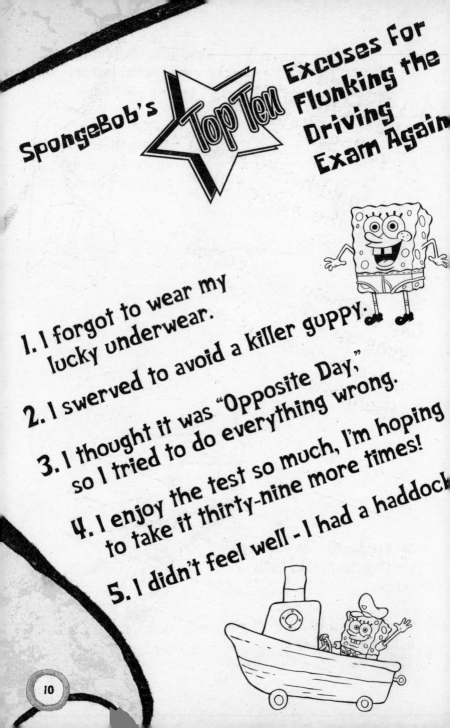

1. I forgot to wear my lucky underwear.

2. I swerved to avoid a killer guppy.

3. I thought it was "Opposite Day," so I tried to do everything wrong.

4. I enjoy the test so much, I'm hoping to take it thirty-nine more times!

5. I didn't feel well – I had a haddock

6. I stopped when I heard the seaweed yelling, "Kelp! Kelp!"

7. I could hardly hear Patrick on the walkie-talkie.

Can you help SpongeBob come up with three more excuses? Write them here:

_____

_____

_____

_____

_____

_____

_____

Mrs Puff: Why are you always late for school?

SpongeBob: They're always ringing the bell before I get here!

Why didn't Mrs Puff believe the Flying Dutchman's excuse?

She could see right through it.

Mr Krabs: Why are you so behind in Krabby Patty orders?

SpongeBob: I don't know, but I'm trying to ketchup!

SpongeBob: Why can't you ever stand still?

Sandy: If I do, I'll go nuts.

Squidward: Why can't you leave me alone?

SpongeBob and Patrick:
You're our favourite
stick-in-the-sand.

SpongeBob's *Top Ten* Excuses For Being Late to Work

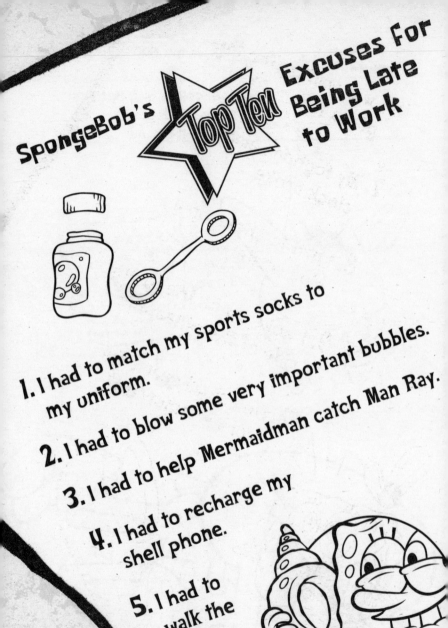

1. I had to match my sports socks to my uniform.

2. I had to blow some very important bubbles.

3. I had to help Mermaidman catch Man Ray.

4. I had to recharge my shell phone.

5. I had to walk the snail.

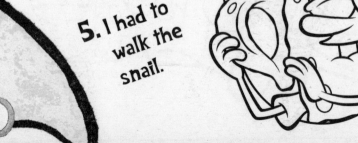

6. I was waiting for the piano tuna.

7. My foghorn alarm clock broke.

8. I had to cheer up a blue whale.

9. I woke up on the wrong side of the pineapple.

10. I'm actually early for work - tomorrow!

KARATE CUTS

Mr Krabs: Why are you doing karate at work?

SpongeBob: I thought I was supposed to punch the time clock!

Mrs Puff: Why are you doing karate at school?

SpongeBob: It's my back-to-school chopping!

Squidward: Why are you doing karate in the kitchen?

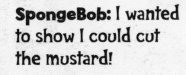

SpongeBob: I wanted to show I could cut the mustard!

Excuuuuuse Me!

Patrick: I'm afraid my son can't go to school today.

Mrs Puff: Oh, that's too bad. And to whom am I talking?

Patrick: This is my father.

Squidward: Why are you blowing bubbles?

SpongeBob: Because I already blew my nose.

21

Salty Answers to Stupid Questions

Customer: Do you sell Krabby Patties?
Squidward: No, we make them laugh.
They're very picklish.

Squidward: Are you going jellyfishing?
SpongeBob and Patrick: No, we're catching
some rays. Stingrays.

SpongeBob: Did you have an accident?
Mrs Puff: No, I purposely crashed the boat so you would ask that question.

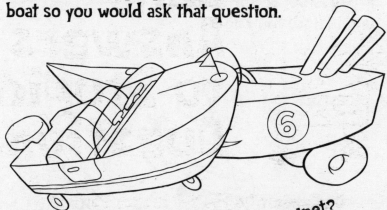

SpongeBob: Are you playing the clarinet?
Squidward: No, I'm tickling it till it laughs.

Mr Krabs: Is that your pet snail?

SpongeBob: Shhhh! Molluscs are people, too, you know.

SpongeBob: Are you asleep?

Patrick: No, I'm using my body to hold this rock down.

Customer: There's a fly on my Krabby Patty!

Squidward: Don't worry, we won't charge you extra for it.

Customer: Are Krabby Patties healthy?

Squidward: I've never heard one complain.

Customer: Will my Krabby Patty be long?

Squidward: No, it'll be round, sir.

Customer: This Krabby Patty tastes funny.

Squidward: Then why aren't you laughing?

Customer: Do you have seaweed salad on the menu?

Squidward: No, I wiped it off!

Mr Krabs: How did you find your Krabby Patty, mate?

Customer: Easy. I just moved the fries and there it was!

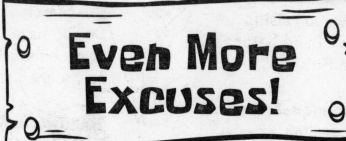

Even More Excuses!

Mr Krabs: Why did you spill sea-onion ice cream on your new Krusty Krab uniform?

SpongeBob: My old one was in the wash!

$

Pearl: Daddy why aren't you paying attention?

Mr Krabs: Um ... how much do I have to pay it?

Mr Krabs: Why are you raising your hand before I'm finished?

SpongeBob: I'm not! I'm hailing a crab.

Squidward: Can you dimwits keep down the noise? I can't even read!

Patrick: Too bad. I've been reading since I was a little starfish.

SpongeBob: Why don't you take the rubbish out?

Patrick: We don't like the same movies!

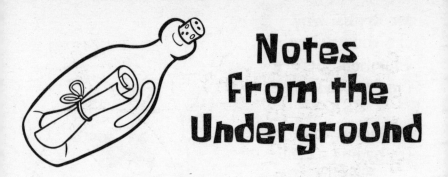

Notes From the Underground

Ahoy, teacher!
Please excuse my darlin'
Pearl from gym class.
She hurt her fin carrying
a bucket o'clams at the
Krusty Krab.

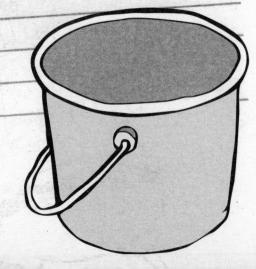

So she shouldn't
be asked to
do any kind
of exercise,
except cheerleading
practice. Or I'll sue
for ever'thing
you've got.

Yours truly,
Mr Krabs

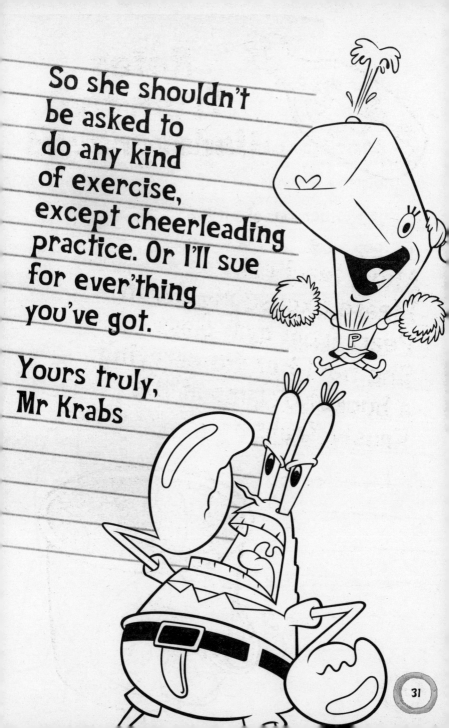

Dear Mrs Puff,

Please excuse my bubble buddy from
missing school.
He was nervous about the
"pop" quiz.

From now on, he'll try not
to be absent.

SpongeBob

from the desk of MRS PUFF

SpongeBob,

I'll give your bubble buddy another chance, but frankly I don't know what you see in him....

Mrs Puff

Dear Mr Krabs,

Please excuse SpongeBob for missing work, but he has been struck down by the dreaded Suds, which cause sniffling, sneezing and complaining.

He must stay in bed for three days, drink plenty of Diet Dr. Kelp and watch Mermaidman and Barnacleboy. This is the only known cure.

Sincerely ,
Dr Fishman

Dear Mrs Puff,

My daughter couldn't take her boating exam because she was just too chicken.

Henrietta Hen

from the desk of MRS PUFF

Eggs-cuses, eggs-cuses!

—Mrs Puff

Patrick's mum: Patrick brought a note home from school.

Patrick's dad: What did it say?

Patrick's mum: They want a written excuse for his presence.

Patrick: The snail ate my homework.

Mrs Puff: But you don't have a snail!

Patrick: It was a stray!

Sandy: Why are you wearing fake muscles?

SpongeBob: The muscles are real – the rest of me is fake.

SpongeBob's **Top Ten** Excuses For Losing the Krusty Krab Talent Show

1. My hands were clammy.

2. Choosing socks that match is a talent!

3. Squidward's better since he switched to electric clarinet.

4. I didn't know Patrick could carry a tuna!

5. I shouldn't have agreed to do a ballet with Plankton.

6. My pineapple's too crowded for more trophies.

7. I can't compete with Patrick - he's a star!

8. I didn't know that was the judge's head.

Can you help SpongeBob come up with two more excuses?

Write them here:

_____

_____

_____

_____

_____

Pearl: Why is money so important
to you?

Mr Krabs: Who ay it'$
$o important?

Policeman: Did you see that sign that
said ONE WAY?

Patrick: But Officer, I'm
only going one way!

Mrs Puff: Why are you late for the first day of school?

SpongeBob: My clock was slow.

Mrs Puff: Do you expect me to believe that?

SpongeBob: You'd be slow, too, if you were running all night.

Mix 'n' Match 'n' EXCUSE ME!

First match a character in
Column A with a problem in
Column B. Then on the next few pages
write an excuse for that character!

Column A	Column B
SpongeBob	waking up late
Squidward	missing an appointment
Patrick	losing a shoe
Mr Krabs	forgetting to make dinner
Pearl	burning a Krabby Patty
Plankton	spilling food on a Krusty Krab customer
Mrs Puff	not writing a thank-you note for a birthday gift
Sandy	driving too fast

Excuses

1. _____ 's excuse for
                (character)

_____ is: _____
          (problem)

_____.
               (excuse)

2. _____ 's excuse for
                (character)

_____ is: _____
          (problem)

_____.
         (excuse)

3. _____'s excuse

(character)

for _____

(problem)

is: _____

(excuse)

_____.

4. _____'s

(character)

excuse for _____

_____

(problem)

is: _____

(excuse)

_____.

5. _____'s excuse for _____

(character)

_____

(problem)

is: _____.

(excuse)

6. _____ 's excuse for
      (character)

_____ is: _____.
      (problem)   (excuse)

7. _____ 's excuse for
      (character)

_____ is: _____.
      (problem)   (excuse)

8. _____ 's excuse for
      (character)

_____
      (problem)

_____

is:_____
      (excuse)

_____

_____.

47

SpongeBob's Favourite Excuse Of All...

Sorry, I was too busy jellyfishing with Patrick!

BOOK OF TRIVIA

This edition published by Parragon in 2013

Parragon
Chartist House
15–17 Trim Street
Bath BA1 1HA, UK
www.parragon.com

Book of Excuses written by Holly Kowitt
Book of Trivia written by David Fain

ISBN 978-1-4723-0752-1

Printed in the UK

BOOK OF TRIVIA

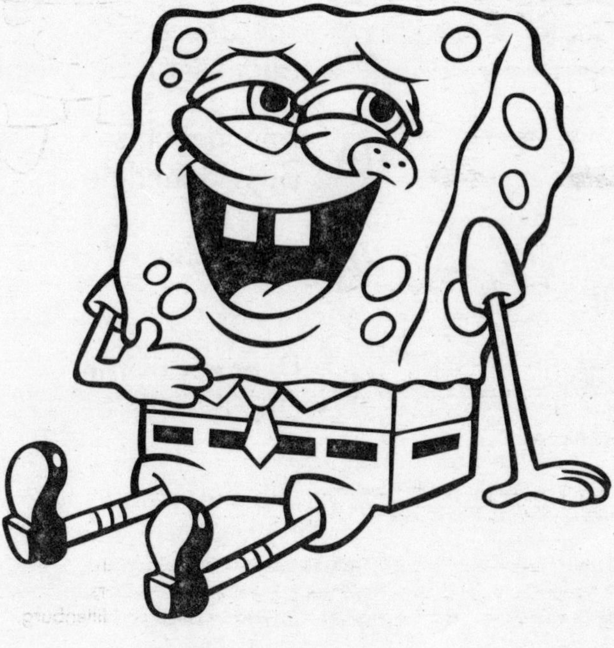

Bath • New York • Singapore • Hong Kong • Cologne • Delhi
Melbourne • Amsterdam • Johannesburg • Shenzhen

TABLE of CONTENTS

Ahoy there, mateys! Here's the rarest sea creature of them all – SpongeBob SquarePants! He may look like an ordinary sponge to you landlubbers, but take my word for it, he's the most unique talking yellow cube filled with holes you'll ever find on the ocean floor – or any floor for that matter.

I'M READY!

Hi! I'm SpongeBob SquarePants! And I'm ready to start another wonderful day here in Bikini Bottom. Whoops! Look at the time! I still have to do my morning workout and feed my pet snail, Gary, before I go to work.

FRIENDS and NEIGHBOURS

I've got lots of neat friends. Let me introduce you to some of them.

Patrick is my best friend. We do everything together: jellyfishing, blowing bubbles, you name it. He also likes sleeping, drooling, and lying dormant under his rock.

Sandy is a land squirrel, so she has to wear a hat full of air and a pressure suit underwater. She's a great surfer and a karate expert, just like me! She's from a faraway place called Texas.

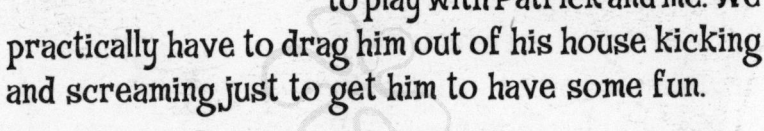

That's my neighbour, Squidward Tentacles. Even though we work together at the Krusty Krab, I never get tired of spending time with him. He practises his clarinet a lot, although he never seems to get any better. He doesn't have time to play with Patrick and me. We practically have to drag him out of his house kicking and screaming just to get him to have some fun.

Mr Krabs is my boss, and the owner of the Krusty Krab restaurant. People say he's cheap, but I consider it an honour to work for the creator of the Krabby Patty! Sometimes I think that maybe I should be paying him!

AROUND
BIKINI BOTTOM

Patrick's rock

two-storey pineapple

Easter Island head

Here's where we live. The pineapple is mine. It has a shell phone, state-of-the-art stuffed animal barbells, and a foghorn alarm clock. Next door is Squidward's Easter Island head, and next to that is Patrick's rock. Every weekend I use my reef blower to keep my yard seashell free.

Howdy, y'all! This is my house, the treedome! It's full of the driest, purest, airyest air in the whole sea! I have all the comforts of home: an exercise wheel, a picnic table, an oak tree and a trampoline.

Ahoy, mateys! An anchor is what me and me daughter, Pearl, call home! My darlin' Pearl is pretty hard to miss, and a pretty miss ta boot! Har! Har!

Daddy, you're embarrassing me! I'm going to cheerleading practice!

She's a whale y'see (takes after her mother that way).

BORN to COOK

Here it is, my work place, the finest eating establishment ever established for eating – the Krusty Krab! Home of that tasty, juicy, scrumptious, warm mouthful of steamy goodness called the Krabby Patty! Would you like fries with that?

Across the street is the Chum Bucket, owned by Mr Krabs's arch-rival, Plankton! With the help of his computer, Karen, Plankton's always trying to steal the Krabby Patty recipe. People say he's evil, but I think he just needs a friend.

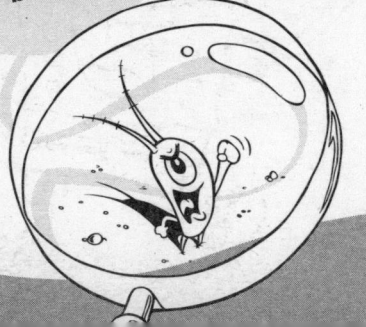

It's not that easy to become a member of the Krusty crew. You really need the expertise to properly prepare the perfect Krabby Patty.

First comes the bun, then the patty, followed by ketchup, mustard, pickles, onions, lettuce, cheese, tomatoes and bun – in that order.

THE RENAISSANCE CEPHALOPOD

Hello, friends, and welcome to my private art gallery. I have conquered all artistic mediums in my pursuit of the perfect self-portrait. Being the only squid of culture in this backward community is a heavy burden, but one I could gladly bear if it weren't for the constant pestering of ... SPONGEBOB SQUAREPANTS! I can't get a moment's peace from that nuisance and his equally annoying friend Patrick!

Do you know they come over every day (and twice on Sundays) to ask me if I want to go jellyfishing? Jellyfishing? Me? Have you ever heard of anything so ridiculous?!

And that's just the beginning! SpongeBob throws me birthday parties when it's not my birthday,

he's always making a racket,

and as if that isn't bad enough, he keeps leaving his underwear on my front lawn!

BUBBLE-BLOWING TECHNIQUE

Wanna blow some bubbles? It only costs 25p. Here's your bubble wand, dipped and ready to go. Remember, it's all in the technique!

* First, go like this.
* Spin around – stop!
* Double-take three times ... one, two, and three.
* Pelvic Thrust – Woo Hoo!
* Stomp on your right foot. (Don't forget it!)
* Now it's time to bring it around town. Bring it around town!
* Then you do this, then this, and this and that and thisandthatandthisandthat!

You can blow bubbles in all sorts of interesting shapes.
Try some of these:

A CUBE

DUCKS   A DANCE PARTNER

A CENTIPEDE   A TUGBOAT

A BUTTERFLY   AN ELEPHANT

You can also whisper messages inside the bubbles
to send to your friends. Just be sure the right
person gets the right message. Or that the message
is from the right person. Or that the message goes
to the person on your right. Or that you don't
forget ... oh, tartar sauce! I forgot who I was
sending this message to!

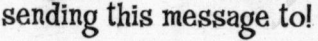

CHAMPIONS
OF THE DEEP

You're just in time for my favourite television show:
The Adventures of MermaidMan! I've got a
genuine imitation copy of his uniform. Patrick says
his young ward, Barnacle Boy, is better, but that's just
because that's who he is when we play superheroes.

They are so
cool! Patrick
and I found out that
MermaidMan and Barnacle
Boy live over at the Shady
Shoals older citizens' home. We
think they're working undercover!

Recently roused from retirement, the aquatic
avengers have launched a new series of
adventures, though now much older (and
considerably less wiser). Watch in awe as they:

Change a lightbulb!

**Wait for the
aquaphone repairman!**

Eat their pies!

**Adjust their
hearing aids!**

Play chess!

**Try to remember where
they parked the invisible
boatmobile!**

BOATING SCHOOL QUIZ

When I'm not working, I go to Mrs Puff's Boating School. I can hardly wait until I get my licence. If only I didn't always get so nervous during the driving exam. Oh well, you know what they say – thirty-eighth time's the charm! (Okay, thirty-ninth!)

Mrs Puff is the best boating teacher I've ever had. Well, actually she's the only boating teacher I've ever had. She's a puffer fish (which means she has her own built-in airbag, which comes in very handy during those driving tests). Let's see how much you know about boating:

1. **The front of the boat is called the**
   a) bow.
   b) porthole.
   c) stern.

2. **The first thing you do when you're about to start the driving test is**
   a) floor it!
   b) put it in drive.
   c) start the boat.

3. **Red means**
   a) floor it!
   b) stop.
   c) make a right turn.

4. **If you see a big anchor in the middle of the road, you should**
   a) floor it!
   b) crash into it.
   c) jump over it.

5. **The second thing you do when you're taking the driving test is**
   a) pop a wheelie.
   b) put it in drive.
   c) cross the finish line.

6. **In boating terms, right is**
   a) starboard.
   b) port.
   c) wrong.

7. **If you see someone on the crossing while you're driving, you should**
   a) get out and help him or her cross the street.
   b) turn around and go the other way.
   c) go upside down.

8. **If your boat has a kitchen onboard it's called**
   a) the keel.
   b) the hall monitor.
   c) the galley.

9. **If you have a walkie-talkie inside your head and someone else is telling you what to do during the driving test, you**
   a) are lucky.
   b) are dreaming.
   c) are cheating.

10. **The final thing you should do when you're taking the driving test is**
   a) watch Mrs Puff being taken away in an ambulance.
   b) cross the finish line.
   c) floor it!

21

SQUIDWARD SEZ

Our pal Squidward is always claiming that he doesn't want to play with SpongeBob and me. We know he's just playing a game where he says the opposite of what he really means (just like on Opposite Day). Let me show you. First he'll talk, and then I'll translate.

WHEN SQUIDWARD SAYS:

"How did I ever get surrounded by such loser neighbours?"

HE REALLY MEANS:

"I have the best neighbours in the world!"

WHEN SQUIDWARD SAYS:

"You're killing me, SpongeBob ... you really are!"

HE REALLY MEANS:

"Do it again!"

WHEN SQUIDWARD SAYS:

"Can we lower the volume, please?"

HE REALLY MEANS:

"Do it again . . . louder!"

WHEN SQUIDWARD SAYS:

"Oh, puh-leez!"

HE REALLY MEANS:

"You're welcome."

WHO SAID IT?

Hear me, surface dwellers! That simpleton starfish isn't the only one around here who knows something about language! I have created a foolproof device that allows me to perfectly imitate the voice of any resident of Bikini Bottom I choose! Don't ask how this will help me to obtain a Krabby Patty – it's far too complicated to explain to your minuscule mentalities. All I need to do is match the phrases with the people who say them – an easy task for an evil genius like me!

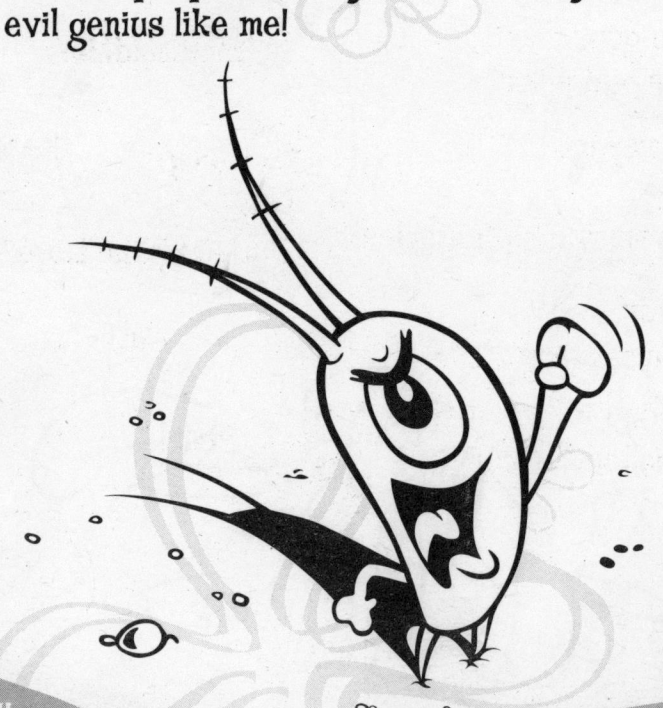

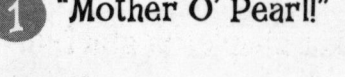

1. "Mother O' Pearl!"
2. "Sea creatures assemble!"
3. "Is it already time to ruin Squidward's day?"
4. "Meow."
5. "Ain't that just the bee's knees?"
6. "You guys want to lift some weights?"
7. "I'm ready!"
8. "Oh, my aching tentacles!"
9. "Daddy, you're embarrassing me!"
10. "Whose turn is it to be hall monitor?"

A. SpongeBob
B. Patrick
C. Sandy
D. Squidward
E. Mr Krabs
F. MermaidMan
G. Gary
H. Larry the Lobster
I. Mrs Puff
J. Pearl

25

MUSSEL BEACH PARTY

This is Mussel Beach, where my friends and I sometimes go to have fun. Everyone has their own favourite things to do here, and at the nearby, wonderful, stinky mud puddle we call Goo Lagoon. I'll let them tell you themselves!

Well, I get really stoked from catching a wave! That's surfing, for all you non-aquatic wannabes. My favourite move is to do a handstand while shooting the tube. That way I can hang ten ... fingers that is! I also enjoy playing Frisbee with my friends, although SpongeBob tends to try catching it with his face!

What I like doing most at Goo Lagoon is lying on the sand and sleeping. Actually I just like lying on the sand and sleeping. I don't even have to be on sand ... or even lying down. I just ... like ... zzz zzz zzz.

Well, if I wasn't always being bothered by certain very annoying people, I would luxuriate in working on my tan at Mussel Beach.

As for me, I like hanging out in the juice bar, singing beach music and playing in the sand. But here are a few activities you want to avoid if you don't want to end up the biggest loser on the beach:

- Getting sand in your buns
- Forgetting your suncream (and getting sunburned)
- Being buried in the sand and getting left behind
- Ripping your pants (repeatedly)
- Pretending to drown

27

MAY I TAKE YOUR ORDER?

THE KRUSTY KRAB, HOME OF THE ONE AND ONLY KRABBY PATTY!

Remember, at the Krusty Krab,

YOU ARE THE CAPTAIN!

SANDWICHES

£2.00

KRABBY PATTY

£2.50

DOUBLE KRABBY PATTY
WITH THE WORKS

KRUSTY COMBO KRABBY PATTY, FRIES AND MEDIUM DRINK

£3.99

£3.00

KRUSTY DELUXE
DOUBLE KRABBY PATTY
WITH THE WORKS AND OYSTER SKINS

CRYING JOHNNIE
KRABBY PATTY
WITH EXTRA ONIONS

£2.25

£1.99

BUBBLE BASS SPECIAL
KRABBY PATTY, HOLD THE PICKLES
(UNDER YOUR TONGUE)

£1.75

MINNOW MEAL
SEANUT BUTTER AND JELLYFISH JELLY
SANDWICH, FRIES AND SMALL DRINK

SIDES

OYSTER SKINS 50P
FRIES £1.25
SEAWEED SALAD £1.50
CORAL BITS £1.95

DRINKS

SALTY SHAKES 99p

DR KELP OR
DIET DR KELP 89p

And don't forget, every Tuesday is Mouthful of
Clams Day! Everyone who shows up with a mouthful
of clams gets a free drink!

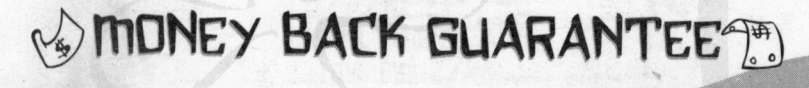

MONEY BACK GUARANTEE

THE SECRETS to SUCCESSFUL JELLYFISHING

Welcome to Jellyfish Fields, where wild jellyfish roam, just waiting to be captured. This is the best place in Bikini Bottom to go jellyfishing. Here are a few pointers for you beginners:

- Bring a good solid net. Be sure to name it. Mine's called "Ol' Reliable."

- Remember, SAFETY FIRST! Always wear your safety glasses.

- Firmly grasp the net.

- Always set the jellyfish free after you've caught it (you wouldn't like being kept in a jar either).

- It helps if you sing "La, la, la" or "Da, da, da, da dum" while you jellyfish.

- Disguise yourself as a piece of coral in order to get close to your prey.

- Watch out for those stingers!

The jellyfish who live in Bikini Bottom are completely different from all other jellyfish in the sea. For example, they make a loud buzzing sound when they swim, they live in hives, and produce a delicious strawberry-flavoured jelly. There's nothing like the taste of natural jelly from a jellyfish.

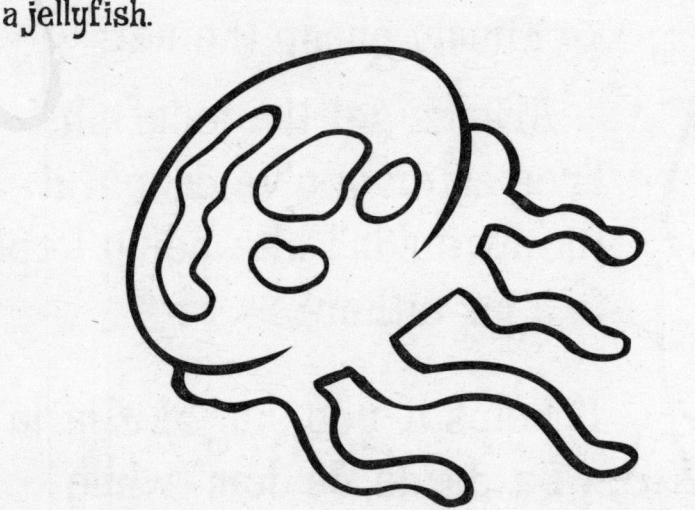

Remember, these jellyfish aren't pets, they're wild animals. They have powerful electrical stingers and use them when angry. They love to dance, and can't resist a good solid beat. But be warned: they don't like clarinet music (at least they don't like the way Squidward plays clarinet music)!

33

SPONGEBOB'S BUSY SCHEDULE

Sometimes I have so much to do it's hard to keep it straight. I'm glad I've got somewhere to write it all down!

Sunday 10
Opposite Day. Be sure to act like Squidward.

Monday 11
Boating Exam today - don't forget to bring apple for Mrs Puff. (Some bandages might not be a bad idea either.)

Friday 15
15th of the month ... Annoy Squidward Day! Call Patrick.

Saturday 16
Squidward's Birthday!

Sunday 17
Annual Jellyfish Convention in Ukulele Bottom. Find snail-sitter for Gary.

Tuesday 19

Ask Squidward to cover as fry cook. Buy Mr Krabs a gift to make up for loss in profits.

Wednesday 20

Squidward's Birthday!

Thursday 21

Glove World Grand Opening! Remind Patrick we need to stand in line all weekend to be sure we are the very first ones inside, just like last year.

Saturday 23

Sign-Up Deadline for Mussel Beach Anchor Throw. Make sure to keep Sandy busy and far away from Goo Lagoon. Prepare Karate ambush?

Sunday 24

Squidward's Birthday!

Tuesday 26

Employee of the Month Judging Begins. Break Squidward's alarm clock.

Wednesday 27

Anniversary of First Day met Sandy. Definitely prepare karate ambush! Pay day. Buy Mr Krabs a sympathy card.

Friday 29

Squidward's Birthday!

SNAIL CARE

Meow!

Okay, I'll tell them, Gary.
Gary wants me to let you
know the most important
information in the care
and feeding of pet snails:

1. Snails need lots of food. They get one can of snail food in the morning and one can at night.

2. Don't let them get salty. Make sure they have plenty of water.

3. They need to be walked twice a day.

4. Snails love to play 'fetch.' Bring something to read, this can take a while.

5. Your pet snail's "meowing" at the moon can annoy the neighbours. Try to keep it to a minimum.

6. Snails are natural-born poets. Encourage their artistic expression.

7. VERY, VERY IMPORTANT: Whatever you do, don't let yourself get accidentally injected with snail plasma.

DANGERS of the DEPTHS

Howdy, y'all. As Bikini Bottom's resident science expert, I'm here to tell y'all about a few sea critters you should give a wide berth to should they ever cross yer path:

Giant Clam. I tussled with one of these rascals myself the first time SpongeBob and I met. They're just big bullies. A few well-placed karate chops will more'n likely send them on their way with their tails betwixt their legs (if they had any legs, that is).

Nematodes (or undersea worms). These hungry little dudes don't look like much, but put a pack of them together and they can gnaw a coral reef down to a stub in ten seconds flat.

The Mother of All Jellyfish. This is the large economy-sized version of those cute little fellers who float out in Jellyfish Fields. But this mamma packs quite a wallop when it comes to stingers. Just ask Squidward.

Anchovies. Just like the nematodes, these tiny little dudes ain't anything to be afraid of in small numbers, but fill a few tour buses with schools of these hungry fish and they're as likely to stampede as look at ya! And to top it off, they're smellier than anything.

Poison Sea Urchins. They're tiny and spiny and make you itch all over.

The Flying Dutchman. Although technically not a critter, he's more of a bogeyman ghost-type varmint. Anyhoo, he's as grumpy as Mr Krabs on payday and twice as ugly, so keep yer distance or he'll steal yer soul!

DID YOU KNOW?

Did you know that in Bikini Bottom:

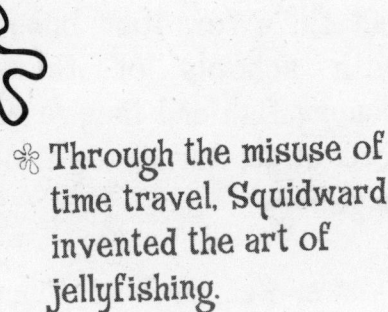

Moss always points to civilisation.

✿ Through the misuse of time travel, Squidward invented the art of jellyfishing.

☺ The specialty of the house at Plankton's restaurant, The Chum Bucket, is Chumbalaya. (No wonder he doesn't have any customers!)

✻ SpongeBob has won the employee of the month award twenty-six months in a row.

☺ The Flying Dutchman haunts the Seven Seas because he was never put to rest (people used his body for a window display after he died).

❋ In the future, everything will be chrome and there will be 486 letters in the alphabet (one for each SpongeTron clone produced).

☉ **Patrick knows a lot about head injuries.**

❋ Mr Krabs has a great sense of smell.

SpongeBob has had the following items inside his head:

*A towel *Plankton

*A walkie-talkie *A lightbulb

(He makes a pretty good disco ball.)

Squidward has a lifetime subscription to **Frown Digest Magazine.**

SpongeBob also plays a mean conch.

Did y'all know that up in the surface world ...

SpongeBob was originally named SpongeBoy, but someone was already using that name, so the "y" became a "b".

✤ SpongeBob SquarePants creator Stephen Hillenburg has a degree in marine biology as well as experimental animation.

✤ Actors Ernest Borgnine and Tim Conway provided the voices for MermaidMan and Barnacle Boy until Borgnine's death in 2012. It was the first time the two had worked together since the 1960s!

🐟 Staff writer Mr Lawrence also performs the voice of Mr Krabs's arch-rival Plankton, the announcer at sporting events in Goo Lagoon, and several others.

❀ Painty the Pirate (seen at the beginning of each SpongeBob SquarePants episode singing the theme song) has the live-action lips of series creator Stephen Hillenburg.

When Stephen Hillenburg took his idea for a cartoon about a sponge to TV bosses, he used an actual aquarium and small models of the characters.

Hollywood star Johnny Depp lent his voice to the character of Jack Kahuna Laguna in the episode 'SpongeBob SquarePants vs The Big One'.

NOW FLIP OVER FOR AN OCEAN OF HILARIOUS EXCUSES

NOW FLIP OVER FOR TANTILISING TRIVIA